ENGLISH TIME
WORKBOOK 3

Melanie Graham
Stanton Procter

OXFORD
UNIVERSITY PRESS

OXFORD
UNIVERSITY PRESS

198 Madison Avenue, New York, NY 10016 USA

Great Clarendon Street, Oxford OX2 6DP England

Oxford New York

Auckland Cape Town Dar es Salaam Hong Kong Karachi
Kuala Lumpur Madrid Melbourne Mexico City Nairobi
New Delhi Shanghai Taipei Toronto

With offices in

Argentina Austria Brazil Chile Czech Republic France Greece
Guatemala Hungary Italy Japan South Korea Poland Portugal
Singapore Switzerland Thailand Turkey Ukraine Vietnam

OXFORD is a trademark of Oxford University Press.

ISBN-13: 978 0 19 436412 6
ISBN-10: 0 19 436412 7

Editorial Manager: Nancy Leonhardt
Senior Editor: Lesley Koustaff
Editor: Paul Phillips
Associate Editor: Christine Hartzler
Senior Production Editor: Joseph McGasko
Associate Production Editor: Nishka Chandrasoma
Elementary Design Manager: Maj-Britt Hagsted
Designer: Ruby Harn
Art Buyer: Elizabeth Blomster
Production Manager: Shanta Persaud
Production Assistant: Zainaltu Jawat Ali

Illustrators: Andrew Shiff, Lynn Jeffery, Julie Durrell, Jane Yamada,
Len Shalansky, Sue Miller, Michelle Dorenkamp, Zina Saunders,
Ann Iosa, George Hamblin, Jim Talbot

Original characters developed by Amy Wummer
Cover illustrations: Jim Talbot
Cover design: Silver Editions

Printing (last digit): 10 9

Printed in Hong Kong.

A. Read and match.

1.

Who's he?
  He's my father.
What's he doing?
  He's laughing.

2.

We're walking. We
  aren't running.

3.

What time is it?
  It's two fifteen.

4.

I like cake. I don't
  like cheese.

B. Read and circle.

1.
He has a | rash.
| cough.

2.
She has a | stomachache.
| fever.

3.
I have | juice.
| chips.

I don't have | candy.
| soda pop.

4.
Does he have | glue?
| tape?

Yes, he does.

5.
Where's the book?

It's | under | the computer.
| next to |

6.
Where's the kite?

It's | on | the desk.
| in |

7.
These | are red flowers.
Those |

8.
What are | those?
| these?

They're | socks.
| shoes.

C. Your turn. Draw and write.

I like _____.

I don't like _____.

A. **Number the sentences in the correct order.**

☐ What does she look like?

☐ Yes! There she is. Thanks.

1 What's wrong?

☐ Is that your mom?

☐ Mom!

☐ She's tall and thin. She's wearing a red dress.

☐ I can't find my mom.

B. **Fill in the blanks. Use some words twice.**

 What's wrong?

 I can't _____ my _____.
                      1   2

 What does _____ look _____?
                     3   4

 _____ wearing a _____ _____. He's _____.
                      5   6   7   8

 Is that your _____?
                       9

 _____! There _____ is. Thanks. Dad!
                      10   11

blue

short

shirt

find

dad

He's

Yes

he

like

A. Read and circle.

1.

turtle

puppy

rabbit

2.

fish

lizard

puppy

3.

bird

fish

mouse

4.

kitten

rabbit

bird

5.

rabbit

kitten

turtle

6.

fish

mouse

bird

7.

mouse

puppy

kitten

8.

lizard

rabbit

fish

B. Read and write.

1. What's this?

It's a _____.

2.

_____

3.

_____

4.

_____

5.  What's that?

It's a _____.

6.

_____

7.

_____

8.

_____

A. Read and check True or False.

	True	False
1. They want a puppy. They don't want a fish.	☐	☐
2. I want a lizard. I don't want a turtle.	☐	☐
3. He wants a rabbit. He doesn't want a kitten.	☐	☐
4. We want a kitten. We don't want a mouse.	☐	☐
5. She wants a turtle. She doesn't want a bird.	☐	☐

B. Look and write.

1. I want _____.

   I don't _____.

2. She _____.

   She _____.

C. Your turn. Draw and write.

What do you want?

_____

_____

_____

A. Does it have short u or long u? Read and circle.

B. Read and circle the words with the same u sound.

1. tune / run / June
2. flute / gum / run
3. blue / duck / up
4. sun / glue / gum
5. run / duck / tube
6. Sue / June / bus

C. Look and write.

1.  glue

2.

3. JUNE calendar

4.

5.

6.

A. Read and connect.

Excuse me.
Can you help me?

Where's the rice?

How about the chips?

Great! Thanks.

Sure.

It's in Aisle 3.
It's next to the bread.

I don't know.
Let's look.

B. Read and circle.

1. Where's the fruit?

   It's | on / under / next to | the bread.

2. Where's the chicken?

   It's | under / in / on | the salad.

3. Where's the cheese?

   It's | in / next to / on | the cake.

Word Time

A. Read and write the letter.

1. cereal __b__   2. fish _____   3. soy sauce _____   4. meat _____

5. shellfish _____   6. eggs _____   7. vegetables _____   8. pasta _____

B. Read and circle.

1. She wants fish and soy sauce.

2. They want pasta and vegetables.

C. Look and write.

1. She has _____.   2. They have _____.

3. He has _____.   4. We have _____.

5. It has _____.   6. I have _____.

A. Read and match.

1. Does he want fish? •

2. Do they want meat? •

3. Does it want pasta? •

• Yes, they do.

• No, he doesn't. He wants eggs.

• No, it doesn't. It wants fish.

B. Look at the picture above. Write.

1. she / meat?

Does she want meat?

No, _____. She _____.

2. they / eggs?

_____

_____

3. he / fish?

_____

_____

C. Read and write.

Do you want fish? _____

A. Read and fill in the chart.

cake   Ted   night   ~~coat~~   blue   glue   ant   feet   ~~cat~~   sick
box   bee   pig   cup   kite   rain   home   bed   run   sock

long a	long e	long i	long o	long u
			coat	

short a	short e	short i	short o	short u
cat				

B. Read and circle the words with long vowel sounds.

1.
May
lake
jam
paint

2.
bee
bed
feet
tea

3.
kite
bike
light
pig

4.
home
boat
box
note

5.
run
blue
Sue
tube

C. Find and circle three words with short vowel sounds.

short a   n s m a p h i h a t y b a g a o t

short e   p e n b y b e d m n e t b e v c t

short i   d b d i g s i t g e y n d s i c k

short o   p t p o t m m o p g i s o c k u n

short u   a p i s n u t s y s u n c b u s r

A. **Unscramble and write the sentences.**

1. to / . / Thursday / Let's / movies / go / the / on

   <u>Let's go to</u> _____

2. How / ? / can't / Friday / I / about / .

   _____

3. busy / I'm / ? / Is / Sorry / okay / Saturday / . / ,

   _____

4. about / What / Sunday / ? / No / .

   _____

5. ! / Sure

   _____

6. ! / good / Sounds

   _____

B. **Write the missing days of the week.**

Sunday

Thursday

Word Time

A. Read and circle.

1.

watch videos
do homework
exercise

2.

clean up
wash the car
have a snack

3.

use a computer
have a snack
listen to music

4.

wash the car
watch videos
clean up

B. Unscramble and write. Then number.

1. istlne ot imsuc

_____

2. ixceerse

_____

3. sue a pucmoetr

_____

4. od meohrkwo

_____

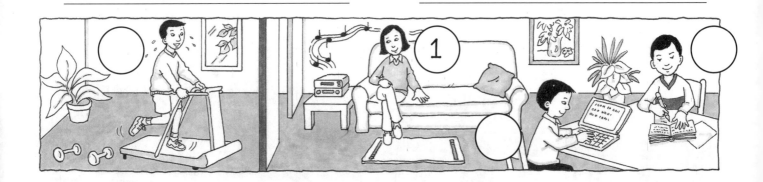

C. Read and write.

1. What's she doing?

_____

_____

2. What's he doing?

_____

_____

A. Read and circle.

1. When | do / does | they do homework?

They do homework | in the morning. / in the evening.

2. When | do / does | she wash the car?

She washes the car | in the afternoon. / at night.

3. When | do / does | it have a snack?

It has a snack | at night. / in the morning.

4. When | do / does | he watch videos?

He watches videos | in the morning. / in the evening.

B. Write the questions and answers.

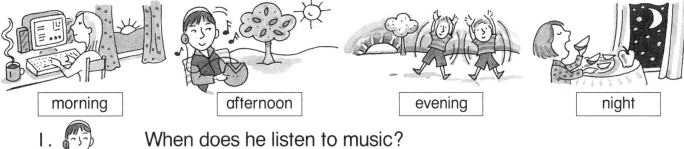

morning   afternoon   evening   night

1. When does he listen to music?

_____

2. When does she use a computer?

_____

3. _____

_____

4. _____

_____

A. Use the code. Look at the pictures and write the initial letters.

1. $\underset{1}{\text{T}} \underset{2}{\text{h}} \underset{3}{\text{e}} \quad \underset{4}{} \underset{5}{} \underset{6}{} \quad \underset{2}{} \underset{7}{} \underset{8}{} \quad \underset{7}{} \quad \underset{6}{} \underset{3}{} \underset{9}{} \underset{9}{} \underset{5}{} \underset{10}{} \quad \underset{11}{} \underset{7}{} \underset{12}{} \underset{13}{} \underset{3}{} \underset{1}{}$.

2. $\underset{1}{\text{T}} \underset{2}{} \underset{3}{} \quad \underset{14}{} \underset{15}{} \underset{3}{} \underset{3}{} \underset{16}{} \quad \underset{9}{} \underset{17}{} \underset{13}{} \underset{3}{} \underset{8}{} \quad \underset{12}{} \underset{7}{} \underset{13}{} \underset{3}{} \quad \underset{7}{} \underset{16}{} \underset{18}{} \quad \underset{19}{} \underset{3}{} \underset{7}{} \underset{1}{}$.

3. $\underset{1}{\text{T}} \underset{2}{} \underset{3}{} \quad \underset{18}{} \underset{15}{} \underset{12}{} \underset{13}{} \quad \underset{22}{} \underset{17}{} \underset{20}{} \underset{3}{} \underset{8}{} \quad \underset{1}{} \underset{2}{} \underset{3}{} \quad \underset{21}{} \underset{7}{} \underset{4}{} \underset{4}{} \underset{17}{} \underset{1}{} \quad \underset{22}{} \underset{15}{} \underset{19}{}$

$\underset{7}{} \underset{16}{} \underset{18}{} \quad \underset{23}{} \underset{5}{} \underset{23}{} \underset{12}{} \underset{5}{} \underset{21}{} \underset{16}{}$.

B. Read the sentences in A. Number the pictures.

A. Read and write ✓.

1.
- [ ] I can't find my brother.
- [ ] How about the popcorn?
- [ ] I can't. How about Friday?

2.
- [ ] He's tall and thin.
- [ ] Where's the pasta?
- [ ] What about Monday?

3.
- [ ] Excuse me. Can you help me?
- [ ] Sorry, I'm busy. Is Tuesday okay?
- [ ] She's wearing a green shirt.

4.
- [ ] I don't know. Let's look.
- [ ] Is that your dad?
- [ ] How about the cereal?

B. Look and write.

Food

eggs _____

_____ _____

_____ _____

Animals

bird _____

_____ _____

_____ _____

A. Read and match. Then number the pictures.

1. Does she want fish? •

2. When do you watch videos? •

3. Does she want cereal? •

4. When do they exercise? •

5. He wants a puppy. •

• I watch videos at night.

• He doesn't want a kitten.

• No, she doesn't. She wants eggs.

• They exercise in the morning.

• Yes, she does.

B. Read and circle.

long a	long e	long i	long o	long u
rat	red	like	dog	duck
lake	see	big	home	bus
Pat	men	night	boat	Luke

short a	short e	short i	short o	short u
bake	Ted	dig	ox	tune
bat	eat	kite	coat	tub
rake	egg	bite	sock	nut

A. Read and circle.

1.
- May I help him?
- Can I help it?
- (May I help you?)

2.
- (Yes, please. One ticket to New York.)
- No, thanks. One ticket to New York.
- Yes, please. One tickets to New York.

3.
- Round trip or one?
- Two ways or round trip?
- One way or round trip?

4.
- Yes, please. When does it leave?
- One way, please. What time does it leave?
- One way, please.

5.
- 2:45. Don't worry!
- 2:45. Please wait.
- 2:45. Please hurry!

B. Read and match.

1. What time is it?
   It's 2:00.

2. What time does it leave?
   2:15.

3. What time is it?
   It's 8:30.

4. What time does it leave?
   9:00.

a.

b.

c.

d.

Word Time

A. Look and complete the puzzle.

Across →

1. 2. 3. 4.

Down ↓

4. 5.

6. 7.

B. Look and write.

1.
This is a _____.
That's a _____.

2.
This is a _____.
That's a _____.

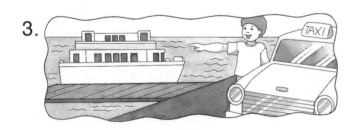
3.

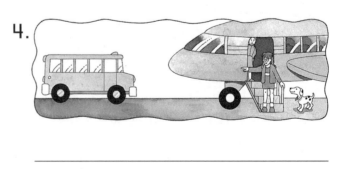
4.

_____

_____

16   Unit 4

A. Read and circle.

1. How does | she / he | go to | school? / work? | She / He | goes to | school / work | by bus.

2. How do | we / they | go to | work? / school? | We / They | go to | work / school | by taxi.

3. How does | she / he | go to | school? / work? | She / He | goes to | school / work | by ferry.

B. Look and write.

1. he / work?

How does he   ?

He goes   .

2. she / school?

_____

_____

C. Your turn. Draw and write.

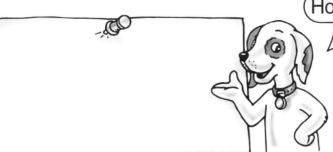

How do you go to school?

_____

_____

Phonics Time

A. Look and write ch, tch, or sh.

1. _____icken

2. pea_____

3. fi_____

4. wa_____

5. _____ell

6.  wi_____

7.  ki_____en

8.  bea_____

9.  _____op

B. Write ch, tch, or sh. Then read and match.

1. The _____icken is eating a pea_____ at the bea_____. •

2. He wants a _____ell. He doesn't want a wa_____. •

3. The wi_____ has a fi_____ in the ki_____en. •

C. Do they both have the same sound? Write ✓ or ✗.

1.

2.

3.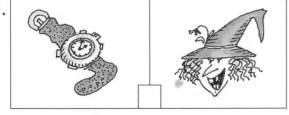

4.

A. Number the sentences in the correct order.

_____ 3 1 Plain Road.

_____ How do you spell "Plain"?

_____ What's your address?

_____ P-l-a-i-n.

_____ Thanks.

_____ Thank you. Have a seat, please.

_____ Pardon me?

_____ 3 1 Plain Road.

B. Fill in the blanks.

| Fish | 423 | spell | s-h | address | What's | telephone number |

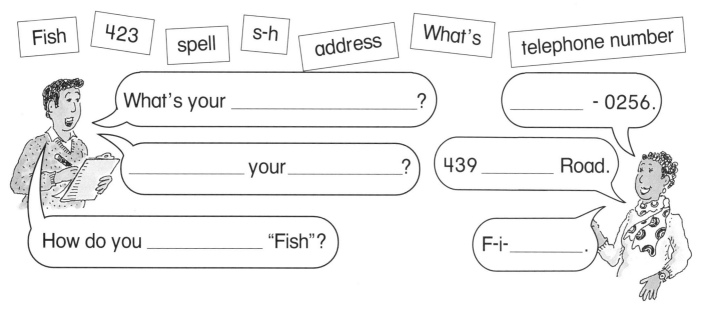

What's your _____?

_____ your _____?

How do you _____ "Fish"?

_____ - 0256.

439 _____ Road.

F-i-_____.

C. Read and write.

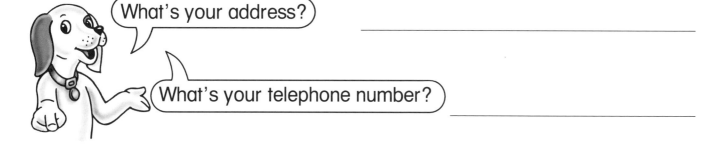

What's your address?

_____

What's your telephone number?

_____

Word Time

A. Read and circle.

1.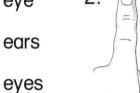
eye
ears
eyes

2.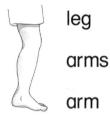
feet
finger
hand

3.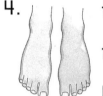
leg
arms
arm

4.
foot
feet
knee

B. Read and write ✓.

1. It has four eyes, two ears, and six legs.

2. It has three legs, three arms, and four eyes.

C. Your turn. Draw and write.

I have two ears.

A. Read and circle.

1.

His
Our | knee | hurt.
hurts.

2.

Their
Her | hands | hurts.
hurt.

3.

My
Your | eye | hurts.
hurt.

4.

Our
Their | feet | hurts.
hurt.

5.

Your
His | finger | hurts.
hurt.

6.

Her
My | ear | hurt.
hurts.

B. Look and write.

What's wrong?

1. _____

2. _____

3. _____

4.  _____

5. _____

6. _____

Phonics Time

A. Follow the words with the voiced th sound.

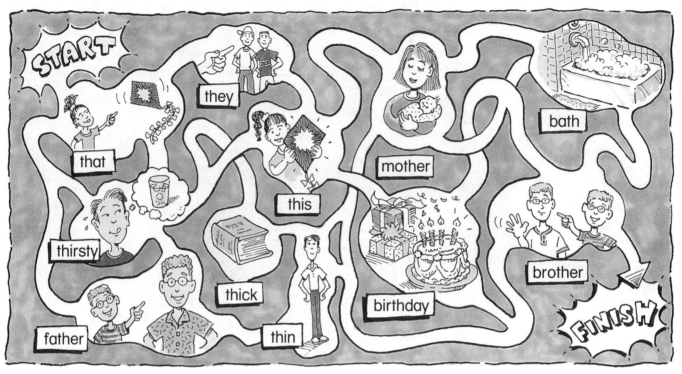

B. Circle the word with the different th sound.

1.	2.	3.	4.	5.
the	thin	thank	father	birthday
mother	that	this	the	these
they	math	bath	thick	thin
think	thirsty	thin	brother	thank

C. Read and match.

1. Beth's brother is thirsty. •

2. This is mine and that's theirs. •

3. She thanks her mother with a hug. •

A. Read and circle.

1.
What are you looking for?
How do you go to school?
What are you doing?

2.
My car! I can't.
My watch! I can't find it.
My coat. It's cold.

3.
Don't worry. I have one.
Don't worry. I'll help you find it.
I'm sorry. I have it.

4.
Okay! Thanks.
Okay. There it is!
Fine, thanks.

5.
What color are they?
Where is it?
What color is it?

6.
It's big!
It's a blue book.
It's red and blue.

B. Fill in the blanks.

What _____ looking for?
1

_____ _____ ! _____ can't find it.
2   3   4

What color _____ your _____ ?
5   6

It's _____ and _____ .
7   8

1	2	3	4	5	6	7	8
is he	Their	kitten	She	are	bird	black	white
are they	Her	puppy	They	am	lizard	blue	blue
is she	His	bird	It	is	puppy	green	pink

A. Circle the odd word.

1. (jacket) / eye / knee / arm   2. bus / taxi / wallet / bicycle

3. kitten / fish / bird / keys   4. cereal / hairbrush / pasta / meat

5. umbrella / rice / shellfish / snack   6. knees / feet / glasses / hands

7. eggs / pasta / lunch box / fish   8. car / ferry / subway / camera

B. Read and find the picture. Write the name.

_____   Sue   _____   _____

1. Sam has a lunch box, a hairbrush, and a jacket.

2. Ben has a cap and a wallet. He's wearing glasses.

3. Sue is wearing glasses. She has an umbrella and a camera.

4. Kate has a hairbrush, keys, and a wallet.

A. Read and write.

1.

Whose glasses are these?

_____ his. _____

2.

_____ are these?

_____

3.

_____

_____

B. Write the questions and answers.

1. / these?   Whose keys are these?
They're his.

2. / this?   _____

_____

3.  / that?      _____

_____

A. Which pictures have the same final y sound? Circle.

candy   baby   cry   bunny   July   Penny   sky

sky   shy   party   bunny   sunny   baby   July

B. Does it have a final y sound? Write ✓ or ✗.

1.	2.	3.	4.	5.	6.
	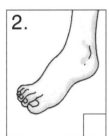				

C. Read and match.

1. Sally eats candy on the ferry. •

2. The bunny goes to a party by ferry. •

3. Jenny and the spy cry and cry. •

4. It's hot and sunny in July. •

a.
b.
c.
d.

A. Read and write.

1. What's his address?

_____

2. What time does it leave?

_____

3. What's she looking for?

_____

4. What's their address?

_____

B. Look and fill in the puzzle. Then draw.

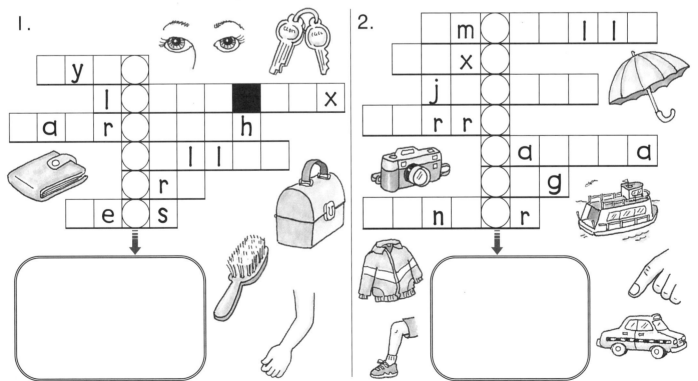

A. Read and find the picture. Then write the name.

May　　　　Kate　　　　Sue　　　　Bess

1. She goes to school by bicycle.
   She has a lunch box. Her arm hurts.
   Her name is _____.

2. She goes to school by bicycle.
   She has a jacket. Her arm hurts.
   Her name is _____.

3. She goes to school by bus.
   She has a jacket. Her hand hurts.
   Her name is _____.

4. She goes to school by bus.
   She has a lunch box. Her hand hurts.
   Her name is _____.

B. Circle the word with a different th or final y sound.

1.
   bath
   thank
   brother

2.
   candy
   baby
   sky

3.
   thin
   these
   thank

4.
   party
   July
   shy

C. Look and write ch, tch, or sh.

1. wi____

2. ____ell

3. pea____

4. ____ellfi____

A. Read and circle.

1.  (How) | many | is | (these)| (?)
   Here | (much) | (are) | this | !

2. They're | off | dollar | each | ,
   There | one | doll | eat | .

3.  Why | ? | That's | cherry | ? | I'll | take | tree | .
   Wow | ! | This | cheap | . | Is | train | three | ,

4. Okay | , | These | tea | dollars | !
   Key | . | That's | three | dollar | .

5.  Hey | ! | Don't | foot | your | change | ?
   Hi | , | Do | forget | you're | cereal | .

6.  Only | ! | There's | a | leg | ,
   Oops | ? | Thanks | I | lot | .

B. Read and write.

1. How much is this?
   It's three dollars.
   _____

2. How much is that?
   _____
   _____

3. How much are these?
   _____
   _____

4. How much are those?
   _____
   _____

A. Read and write ✓ or ✗.

1. This is medicine.

2. This is makeup.

3. This is shampoo.

4. That's soap.

5. That's money.

6. This is toothpaste.

7. That's sunscreen.

8. That's film.

B. Look and write.

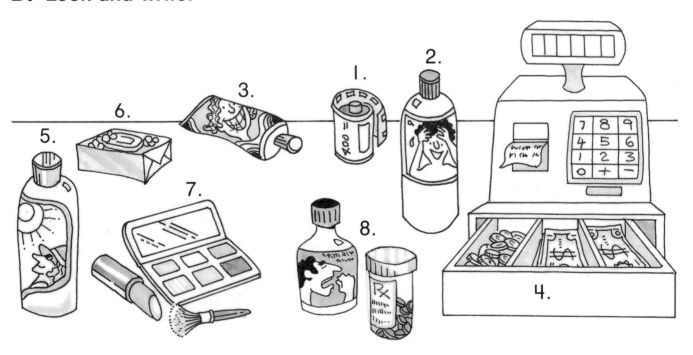

1. _____ 2. _____ 3. _____ 4. _____

5. _____ 6. _____ 7. _____ 8. _____

A. Read, circle, and match.

1. I have some | film.
money. | I don't have any | soap.
shampoo. •

2. I have some | soap.
shampoo. | I don't have any | film.
soap. •

3. I have some | soap.
sunscreen. | I don't have any | medicine.
money. •

B. Look and write.

1. They _____ .
2. She _____ .
3. I _____ .
4. He _____ .

C. Your turn. Draw and write.

What do you have?

_____
_____

A. Do they both have the same final s sound? Write ✓ or ✗.

ducks	girls	cats	cups	trees	bees

dogs	peas	bats	caps	bags	socks

B. Do the words with final s have the same final s sound? Write ✓ or ✗.

1. The cats have cups and bats. ☐

2. The bees and dogs see the trees. ☐

3. The girls have books, peas, and dogs. ☐

C. Circle the word with a different final s sound.

1.
cats
bats
bees
tops

2.
ducks
cups
bags
cats

3.
girls
socks
beets
bats

4.
cups
nuts
caps
cubs

5.
bees
tops
rats
socks

A. Read and match. Then number the pictures.

1. Hey! Don't do that! •   • Oh, I see it. Thanks.

2. Don't litter! Use the trash can. •   • What?

3. It's over there. It's under the tree. •   • I'm sorry. Where is it?

B. Unscramble, write, and match.

1. | TV | the | Wash | Don't | . | car | watch | ! | •

_____

a. •

2. | . | music | to | Clean | ! | listen | Don't | up | •

_____

b. •

3. | snack | Don't | Exercise | have | a | ! | . | •

_____

c. •

4. | ! | climb | a | Don't | Do | tree | . | homework | •

_____

d. •

A. Look and write.

grass	snow	sand
mountains		trees
rivers	wildlife	trails

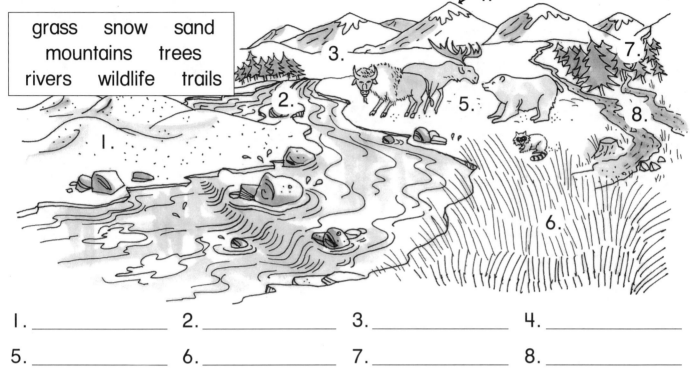

1. _____ 2. _____ 3. _____ 4. _____

5. _____ 6. _____ 7. _____ 8. _____

B. Look, read, and write ✓ or ✗.

1.

snow ☐

2.

grass ☐

3.

trails ☐

4.

trees ☐

5.

wildlife ☐

6.

rivers ☐

7.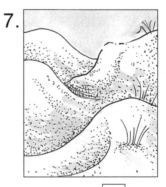

sand ☐

8.

mountains ☐

A. Read and write the letter.

1.

2.

3.

4.

a. There are some trees.
There aren't any trails.

b. There are some mountains.
There isn't any grass.

c. There's some snow.
There isn't any sand.

d. There's some wildlife.
There aren't any rivers.

B. Compare the pictures. What's different? Write three sentences about picture 2.

1.

2.

There's some snow. There aren't any trees. _____

_____

_____

_____

Phonics Time

A. Read and circle the words with the final es sound.

keys   pencil cases   witches   bushes   bees   ducks   bags

apples   beaches   books   oranges   sandwiches   trees

boxes   glasses   buses   cups   peaches   dogs   foxes

B. Read and match.

1. I want peaches and oranges. I don't want eggs.•

a.
•

2. There are glasses under the bushes.•

b.
•

3. The witches have pots and cups.•

c.
•

4. He has some bags. He doesn't have any cats.•

d.
•

C. Does it have the final es sound? Write ✓ or ✗.

1.

2.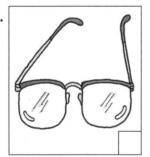

3.

4.

5.

6.

7.

8.

A. Number the sentences in the correct order.

_____ No, thanks. I don't like cookies.

_____ Mm. That sounds good.

_____ Do you want a chocolate chip cookie?

_____ What about some strawberry ice cream?

_____ I'm hungry!

_____ Me, too. Let's have a snack!

B. Look and write.

1.  He wants cookies. He doesn't want cereal.

2.  _____

3. _____

4.  _____

C. Your turn. Read and write.

When do you have a snack?   What do you eat?

_____

_____

_____

Word Time

A. Look and write.

| pickles |
| instant noodles |
| salt |
| mushrooms |
| tofu |
| pepper |
| hot sauce |
| bean sprouts |

There's some…

_____

_____

_____

_____

There are some…

_____

_____

_____

_____

B. Look at A. Fill in the puzzle.

What's the mystery food?

_____

A. Read and write ✓.

1. Is there any tofu?

☐ Yes, there is.
☐ No, there isn't.

2. Are there any pickles?

☐ Yes, there are.
☐ No, there aren't.

3. Is there any salt?

☐ Yes, there is.
☐ No, there isn't.

B. Look and write.

1. <u>Are there</u> _____

_____ **?**

2.  _____

_____

3.  _____

_____

4. _____

_____

5.  _____

_____

6.  _____

_____

A. Circle and write br, gr, or pr.

1.  pr / gr   ____een

2.  br / gr   um____ella

3.  gr / br   ____apes

4.  br / pr   ____own

5.  gr / pr   ____etty

6.  pr / br   ____ize

7.  pr / gr   ____esent

8.  gr / br   ____ead

B. Look, read, and match.

1.    • Ivy gives her grandmother a present.

2.    • I have a green umbrella!

3.    • My grandfather has a prune and a grape.

4.    • I eat brown bread at night.

C. Do they both have the same consonant blend? Write ✓ or ✗.

1.

2.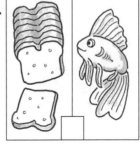

3.

4.

A. Read, check, and write the response.

1.

☐ Don't forget your change.
☐ Don't do that!

Oops! Thanks a lot.

2.

☐ How much are those?
☐ How much are these?

_____

3.

☐ What time is it?
☐ Where is it?

_____

4.

☐ Do you want some pickles?
☐ Do you want some ice cream?

_____

B. Match and write.

1. sun • • work _____

2. wild • • room _____

3. mush • • brush _____

4. hair • • life   wildlife _____

5. tooth • • screen _____

6. home • • paste _____

7. hot • • box _____

8. instant • • sprouts _____

9. bean • • sauce   hot sauce

10. lunch • • noodles _____

11. trash • • cream _____

12. ice • • can _____

Review 3

A. Look and write.

1. _____ mountains. _____ trees.

2. _____ toothpaste. _____ shampoo.

3. _____ money. _____ sunscreen.

4. _____ salt? _____

B. Do they both have the same final sound (es or s)? Write ✓ or ✗.

 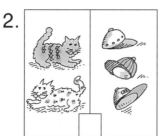  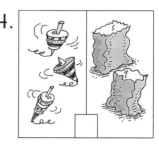

C. Match.

A. Read, circle, and match.

1.

Look	?	Whose	water	are	this	?
Listen	!	Where	wallet	is	that	.

Maybe	I'm	here	,	Let	answer	,
Mother	it's	hers	.	Let's	ask	.

2.

Excuse	me	?
That's	her	.

Why	?
Yes	!

Are	this	your	bag	?
Is	that	you	wallet	.

3.

No	,	it	is	!	Thank	us	too	much	?
Yes	.	it	hers	.	Think	you	so	many	!

We're	welcome	.
You're	wallet	,

B. Read and write.

1. Is this her cap?

_____

2. Are these her glasses?

_____

3. Are these their keys?

_____

Word Time

A. Read and match.

1.

2.

3.

4.

restaurant   department store   bakery   movie theater

museum   hospital   drugstore   bookstore

5.

6.

7.

8.

B. Read and write.

1. Is this a restaurant?

No, it isn't. It's a _____

_____ .

2. Is this a museum?

_____

_____

3. Is this a bookstore?

_____

_____

4. Is this a bakery?

_____

_____

Practice Time

A. Look at the chart. Write.

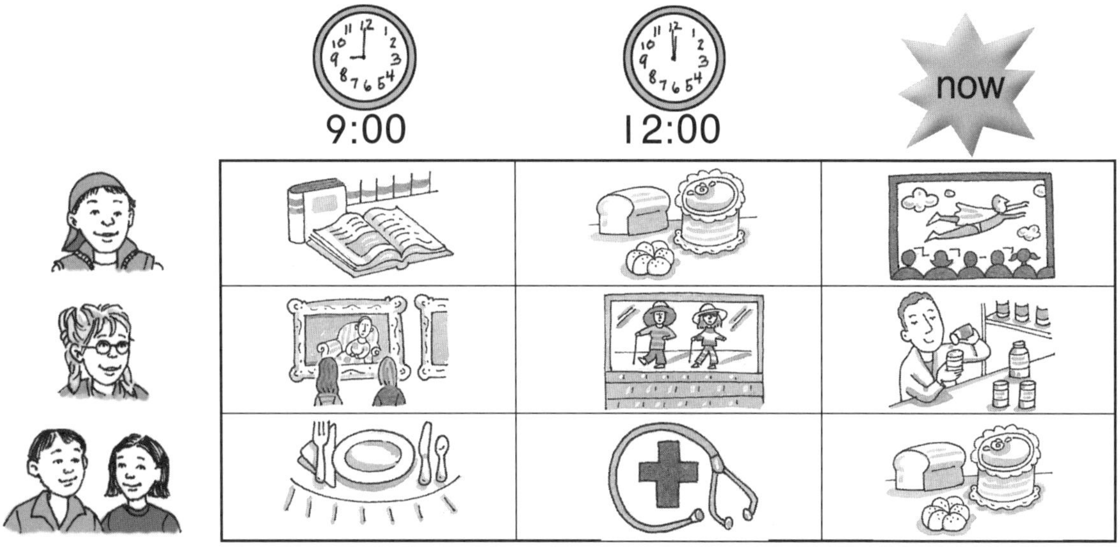

1. 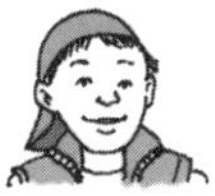 / 12:00 He was at ____________ the ____________.

2. 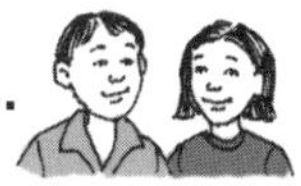 / 9:00 They were ____________ ____________.

3. 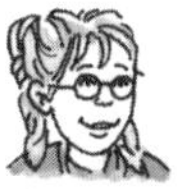 / now She is ____________ ____________.

4. 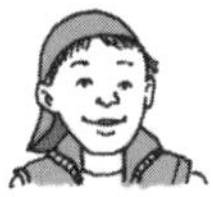 / 9:00 ____________ ____________

B. Look and write.

1. 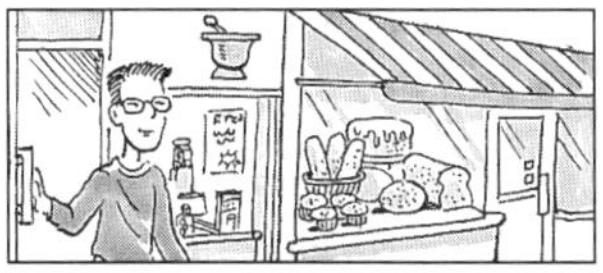 He was ____________.
He wasn't ____________.

2. 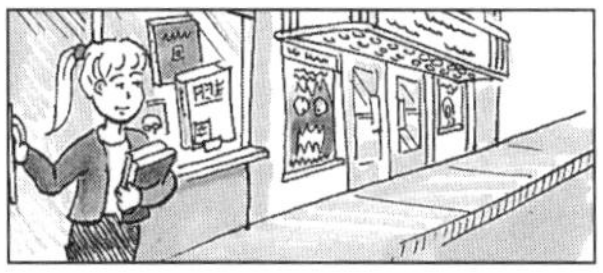 She ____________.
____

3. 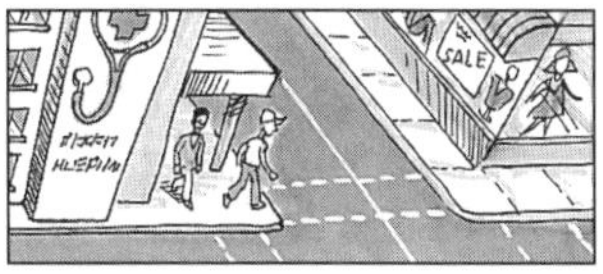 They ____________.
____

4. 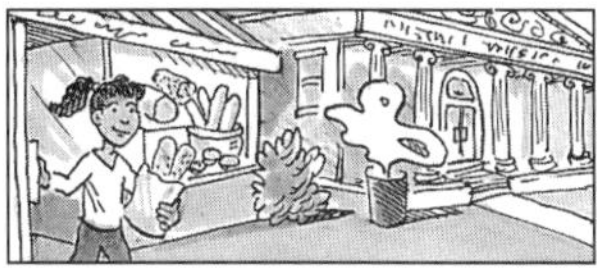 She ____________.
____

A. Look and write cr, dr, or tr.

1.

_____uck

2.

_____eam

3.

_____ess

4.

_____ee

5.

_____y

6.

_____eek

7.

_____ain

8.

_____aw

B. Write cr, dr, or tr. Then read and match.

1. The _____ab wants a _____uck and a _____ain. •

a.

2. The _____ee is next to the _____ugstore. •

b.

3. I _____y on my _____ess. •

c.

4. That's a _____ee. This is a _____eek. •

d.

A. Read and write the letter.

_____ 1. I'm bored.
      So am I. Let's play soccer.

_____ 2. Dad! We're going outside.
      Remember, you have to do your homework.

_____ 3. I know, Dad.
      Be back at six.

_____ 4. All right. Bye!
      Bye, kids. Have fun!

B. Look and write.

| thirsty |
| hungry |
| cold |
| hot |

1. I'm _____.

2. _____

3. _____

4. _____

A. Read and circle.

1.

bathroom

yard

bedroom

2.

dining room

basement

hall

3.

kitchen

living room

bathroom

B. Look at Ted's house. Label the rooms.

1. __bedroom__

2. _____

3. _____

4. _____

5. _____

6. _____

7. _____

8. _____

C. Your turn. Draw your house. Label the rooms.

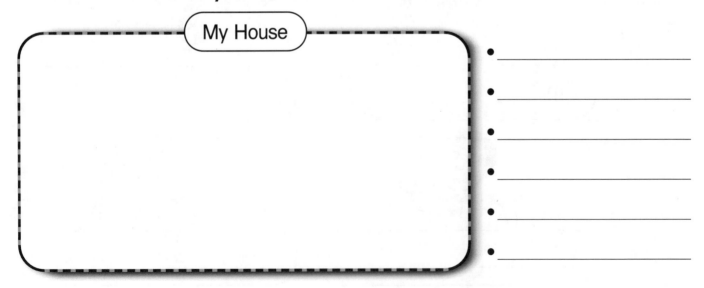

My House

• _____

• _____

• _____

• _____

• _____

• _____

A. Read and write.

1.  Were they in the yard?

__Yes, they were.__

_____

2.  Was she in the bathroom?

_____

_____

3.  Was he in the kitchen?

_____

_____

4.  Was she in the hall?

_____

_____

B. Write the questions and answers.

1. Was she in the bedroom?

_____

_____

2. Was he in the hall?

_____

_____

3. Was she in the kitchen?

_____

_____

4. Was he in the yard?

_____

_____

5.  _____

_____

Yes, _____ .

6.  _____

_____

Yes, _____ .

Phonics Time

A. Circle and write.

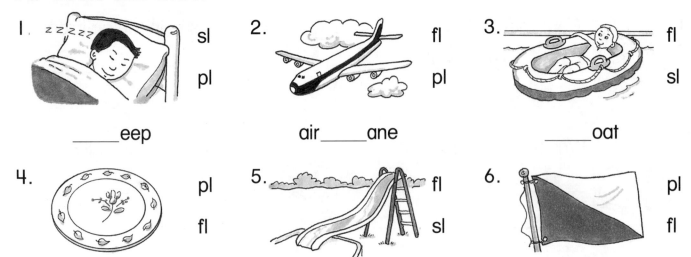

1. sl / pl
   _____eep

2. fl / pl
   air_____ane

3. fl / sl
   _____oat

4. pl / fl
   _____ate

5. fl / sl
   _____ide

6. pl / fl
   _____ag

B. Look, read, and check True or False.

	True	False
1. The cat is playing with a slug.	☐	☐
2. The man is sleeping.	☐	☐
3. There are flowers on the table.	☐	☐
4. There is a plate on the slide.	☐	☐

Now write your own sentence. Then check True or False.

_____   ☐   ☐

Unit 11

A. Unscramble, write, and number.

_____ | this | 245-8769 | Is | ? |

_____

_____ | okay | That's | . | . | Good-bye |

_____

_____ | . | Sorry |

_____

_____ | Is | ? | Hello | Ted | please | ? | there | , |

_____

_____ | sorry | . | I'm | You | number | have | wrong | the | . |

_____

_____ | it | isn't | . | No | , | is | This | 245-8768 | . |

_____

B. Read and match.

1. What are you looking for?
   My pencil. •

2. Is this your pencil?
   No, it isn't. It's hers. •

3. How about this pencil? Is this your pencil?
   Yes, it is! Thanks. •

A. Read and circle.

1.

   brush my teeth
   wash my hands
   wash the car

2.

   watch videos
   play basketball
   play video games

3.

   bake cookies
   make a sandwich
   call a friend

4.

   dance
   practice the piano
   brush my teeth

5.

   wash my hands
   practice the piano
   ride a bike

6.

   call a friend
   clean my room
   do homework

7.

   bake cookies
   dance
   play video games

8.

   watch TV
   practice the piano
   call a friend

B. Write the questions and answers.

1. What's she doing?

   She's baking cookies.

2. What's he doing?

   _____

3. _____

   _____

4. _____

   _____

A. Write.

1. call a friend → _____called_____ a friend

2. bake cookies → _____ cookies

3. wash my hands → _____ my hands

4. brush my teeth → _____ my teeth

5. practice the piano → _____ the piano

6. play video games → _____ video games

7. clean my room → _____ my room

8. dance → _____

Now circle the words.

c	b	t	u	p	r	a	c	t	i	c	e	d
l	a	e	i	p	g	h	i	c	f	e	n	a
e	b	l	m	l	e	a	s	h	e	o	k	n
a	y	s	w	a	s	h	e	d	p	c	l	c
n	p	q	e	y	w	h	f	j	u	a	v	e
e	s	g	a	e	i	w	a	s	l	l	g	d
d	n	u	y	d	o	m	e	r	k	l	b	x
a	b	r	u	s	h	e	d	i	a	e	j	r
y	s	o	r	r	i	y	c	k	o	d	a	p
r	t	v	w	b	a	k	e	d	z	i	t	n

B. Your turn. Read and write.

What did you do today?

_____

_____

A. Look and write sm, sn, or sp.

1.

____ake

2.

____oke

3.

____eeze

4.

____ider

5.

____ell

6.

____ile

7.

____ell

8.

____ow

B. Write sm, sn, or sp. Then read and number the pictures.

1. The ____ake and the ____ider are ____eaking English.

2. Mr. ____ith ____eezed at the ho____ital.

3. Kate is eating bean ____routs in the ____ow.

4. Sam ____elled the rose and ____iled.

A. Connect the conversations.

1. Whose camera is that?
2. I'm bored.
3. Is Jay there, please?

I'm sorry. You have the wrong number.

Maybe it's his. Let's ask.

So am I. Let's play soccer.

Is this 481-7204?

Dad! We're going outside.

Is this your camera?

Be back at 4:00.

No, it isn't.

Yes, it is. Thanks.

B. Circle the odd words. There are two in each line.

1. | museum | bakery | drugstore | money | kitchen | bookstore |

2. | makeup | bedroom | yard | hall | dance | dining room |

3. | call a friend | watch videos | dance | bakery | bake cookies | yard |

4. | movie theater | watch TV | department store | hospital | museum | bake cookies |

5. | basement | bathroom | living room | film | practice the piano | bedroom |

6. | clean my room | yard | wash my hands | brush my teeth | bathroom | dance |

A. Read and check True or False.

			True	False
1.		She was at the museum. She practiced the piano.	☐	☐
2.		He was in the bathroom. He brushed his teeth.	☐	☐
3.		I was at the movie theater. I called a friend.	☐	☐
4.		She was in the bedroom. She baked cookies.	☐	☐

B. Write cr, fl, pl, sl, or sm. Then match.

1. The _____ug is _____oating in the _____eek. •

2. The _____ab ate a _____um and a _____ower. •

3. Craig washed his _____ate and _____iled. •

a.

b.

c.

A. Read the questions. Write the answers.

1.  What does she look like?

   She's _____

   _____ .

2.  Where are the bananas?

   They're _____

   _____ .

3.  How much are these? $2 EACH

   They're _____

   _____ .

4.  Whose lunch box is this?

   Maybe _____

   _____ .

B. Read the answers. Write the questions.

1. _____

   I can't find my mom!

2. _____

   Yes, please. One ticket to New York.

3. _____

   It's red and white.

4. _____

   31 Plum Road.

Word Time Review

A. Find and circle the words.

1.

2.

3.

4.

5.

```
b c r o k p e p p e r e f p a s t a i e
a e l a s m r u t d i r c y w z o c n p
k g d p p f i n g e r h w o c b o o l e
e c b r l o v g e q u k a r m o n e n l
r t s u o l u l s h e t b l o o s a n o
y x i t l o j a c k e t l a u a n f c e
a h i r v i m s t p v c e s s q h e o k
r p h a r m e s x i v o t r e y e s y i
m e d i c i n e x s o a p e t t i m p t
a e s n o e e s b c v p e l p c f h i t
f b a q o u r s l m f t r e e s l a i e
y a i t i y t k e y s m n o p f e e t n
c a r h a l w u n d e l m h a n d s o n
p e d j k d a n c e k a n e y s t j y j
```

6.

7.

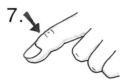

8.

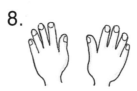

9.

10.

11.

12.

13.

14.

15.

16.

17.

18.

19.

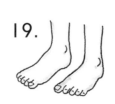

20.

A. Read and match.

1. I want a puppy. •   • They exercise at night.

2. Does she want vegetables? •   • I don't want a turtle.

3. When do they exercise? •   • I go to school by car.

4. How do you go to school? •   • Yes, she does.

5. Her foot hurts. •   • It's his.

6. Whose jacket is this? •   • Her hands hurt.

B. Read and match.

1. He has some money. •   • He doesn't have any shampoo.

2. There's some snow. •   • No, he wasn't. He was at the museum.

3. Is there any hot sauce? •   • There isn't any grass.

4. We were at the hospital. •   • We weren't at the bakery.

5. Was he at the department store? •   • Yes, there is.

6. She called a friend. •   • She didn't clean her room.

Phonics Time Review

A. Circle the words you can read.

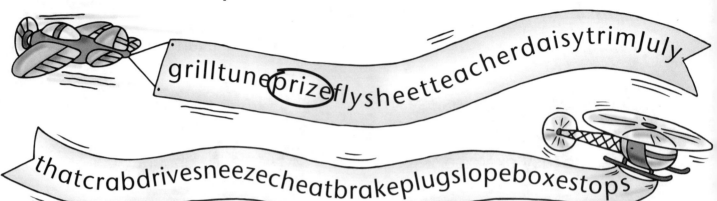

grilltune**prize**flysheetteacherdaisytrimJuly

thatcrabdrivesneezecheatbrakeplugslopeboxestops

B. Do both begin with the same consonant blend? Write ✓ or ✗.

C. What sound does it have? Match.

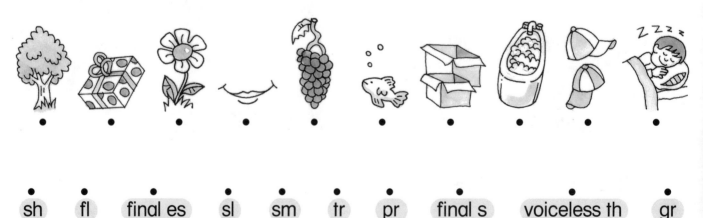

sh   fl   final es   sl   sm   tr   pr   final s   voiceless th   gr